SALEM'S SPIRITS

and Other Hauntings of New England

by Megan Cooley Peterson

CAPSTONE PRESS
a capstone imprint

Capstone Captivate is published by Capstone Press, an imprint of Capstone.
1710 Roe Crest Drive
North Mankato, Minnesota 56003
www.capstonepub.com

Library of Congress Cataloging-in-Publication Data is available on the Library of Congress website.
ISBN: 978-1-4966-8374-8 (library binding)
ISBN: 978-1-4966-8425-7 (eBook)

Summary: Each region of the U.S. has its fair share of hauntings, but maybe none more so than New England. There, the ghosts of accused witches are said to linger in Salem. Haunted hotels are scattered throughout Massachusetts, New Hampshire, and Connecticut. Tormented spirits are reported to reign over what was once Danvers State Hospital. New England might be as rich in ghosts as it is in history. Between these pages, readers will find just the right amount of scariness for a cold, dark night.

Quote Sources
p.12, "The Witchcraft Trial of Giles Corey." History of Massachusetts, Oct. 12, 2011.

Editorial Credits
Editor: Renae Gilles; Designer: Sara Radka; Media Researcher: Morgan Walters; Production Specialist: Katy LaVigne

All internet sites appearing in back matter were available and accurate when this book was sent to press.

Printed and bound in the USA.
PA117

TABLE OF CONTENTS

Words in **bold** are in the glossary.

HAUNTED NEW ENGLAND

New England is said to be the most haunted part of the United States. People report stories of ghostly witches and eerie happenings all over the area. Are you brave enough to visit?

The northeastern part of the United States is called New England. Maine, Vermont, New Hampshire, Massachusetts, Rhode Island, and Connecticut make up this region. Most of New England was among the original 13 **colonies**. It is the oldest part of the United States.

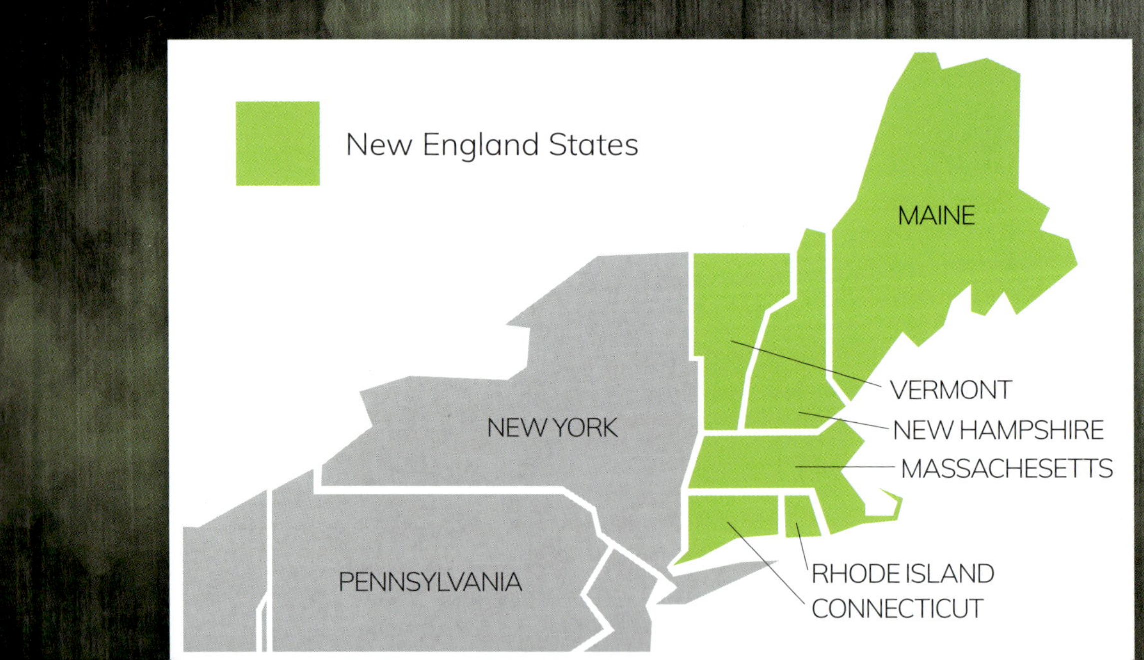

Stratford Shoal is a reportedly haunted lighthouse off the coast of Connecticut in New England.

CHAPTER 1

THE SPIRITS OF SALEM

In 1692, a darkness settled over Salem, Massachusetts. Many young girls in the village suddenly began acting strangely. They said villagers were using witchcraft to hurt them. The villagers said they were innocent. Soon, hundreds of townspeople were locked up. Many were **convicted** in unfair trials. That year, 19 men and women were hanged. One of the young girls later said she had lied about what happened. Today, most historians believe the girls were lying.

The accused did not have help in court and had to defend themselves.

Young girls were among those accused of witchcraft.

TIMELINE OF THE SALEM WITCH TRIALS

- **January 1692**—Girls in Salem Village begin acting strangely.

- **February 29, 1692**—The girls accuse three women of witchcraft. The women are arrested.

- **March 23, 1692**—The 4-year-old daughter of accused witch Sarah Good is arrested for witchcraft. She spends months in prison.

- **June 10, 1692**—Bridget Bishop is hanged.

- **September 22, 1692**—Eight convicted witches are hanged. They are the last to die.

Some people think the spirits of the accused witches who died might still haunt Salem. On a dark October night in 2006, a man named Mike and his girlfriend entered the Old Burying Point Cemetery. It is the oldest cemetery in Salem. The temperature dropped as they moved deeper into the cemetery. Mike said it dropped at least 20 degrees. His skin broke out in goosebumps. His girlfriend suddenly couldn't breathe. She said something—or someone—pushed her. She ran from the cemetery. He took a quick photograph before fleeing. As soon as he snapped the photo, the camera's battery died.

Mike developed the photograph a few days later. What he saw took his breath away. Near a gravestone, a ghostly face rose out of the grass. Mike said he didn't edit the photo. He believes it was a ghost.

WITCH MEMORIAL

None of those hanged during the trials are buried at Old Burying Point. But in 1992, a **memorial** was dedicated to them at the cemetery. The memorial features stone benches. The benches list the names of those who lost their lives.

Judge Jonathan Corwin served as a judge during the Salem Witch Trials. Corwin came from a wealthy English family. He first worked as a shipping **merchant**. Later, he became a judge. After the trials, some judges apologized for their roles. Corwin never apologized.

There were so many witch trials in the Salem area that a special court was formed to handle the cases.

The Corwin House is the only building associated with the witch trials that is still standing.

Corwin's home still stands in Salem. Today, it is a museum. Many people believe it's haunted by the ghosts of the hanged witches. People report being touched by unseen hands. They feel cold spots. They hear ghostly children. Many of Corwin's children died when they were very young. Some even say Jonathan Corwin himself haunts his former home.

A brick mansion on Washington Street is said to be the most haunted place in Salem. Sheriff George Corwin once lived on the land. He was Judge Jonathan Corwin's nephew. George Corwin put an accused witch to death.

The Joshua Ward House was one of the first brick houses in Salem.

His name was Giles Corey. Corey refused to tell the court whether he was innocent or guilty. Corwin piled heavy stones on Corey's body until Corey died. Corey's last words were "I **curse** you and Salem!"

Corwin died four years later of a heart attack. **Legend** says his family buried him in his basement. The home was later torn down. Shipping merchant Joshua Ward built his home in its place in 1784.

Today, the Joshua Ward House is a hotel. Some say Corwin's ghost decided to stick around. Visitors have reported being choked by invisible hands while in the basement. Some believe Giles Corey also haunts the house. People say his ghost knocks over trash cans and throws books.

Giles Corey was in his 80s when accused of witchcraft.

CHAPTER 2

VERMONT'S HAUNTED BRIDGE

Beware when driving across Emily's Bridge in Stowe, Vermont. This covered bridge is said to be haunted. According to stories, a young woman named Emily died there in the 1800s. She rode her horse to the bridge to meet her fiancé. But she was thrown from her horse and died.

Emily's Bridge has been a ghostly hot spot ever since. Unseen hands are said to scratch cars that cross the bridge. A girl's scream rings out when no one is around. Some people are brave enough to walk onto the bridge. Many have reported feeling something brush up against them. Could it be Emily's ghost?

Many people will only cross Emily's Bridge during the daytime. They fear her ghost comes at night.

FREAKY FACT

There is no written evidence that Emily ever existed. Her story might be made up.

CHAPTER 3

THE LIZZIE BORDEN HOUSE

A murder shook the town of Fall River, Massachusetts, in 1892. On August 4, police arrived at the Borden House on 2nd Street. They found the bodies of Andrew and Abby Borden. Both had been killed with an ax. Andrew's daughter, 32-year-old Lizzie, was the main **suspect**.

Andrew had remarried in 1865. Stories say Lizzie never liked her stepmother. The police questioned Lizzie. Lizzie said she was outside at the time of the murders. The maid was also there that day. She said she was napping in the attic and heard nothing. Lizzie was eventually charged with murder. A **jury** found her not guilty. To this day, no one knows who killed the Bordens.

FREAKY FACT

Lizzie and her sister, Emma, got much of Andrew's money when he died. Some say Lizzie might have killed her father and stepmother for the money.

Lizzie Borden

The Bordens purchased their large house in 1872.

A portrait of Lizzie Borden hangs on a wall of the house where she once lived.

Stays at the Lizzie Borden Bed and Breakfast include historical tours and ghost-hunting events.

Today, the house the Bordens lived in is an inn. It is called the Lizzie Borden Bed and Breakfast. The ghosts of Lizzie, Andrew, and Abby are said to haunt the inn. Ghost-like mists float in the bedroom where Abby died. Rocking chairs are said to rock on their own. A ghostly cat has been spotted. It wanders the property. Guests have reported the smell of tobacco when no one was smoking. Unseen hands reach out and touch people.

In 2017, two sisters spent the night in the room where Abby died. Suddenly, a fire alarm blasted them awake around 3:00 a.m. The inn's chef told them that the alarm went off every couple of months. And it always happened around 3:00 a.m. Some ghost hunters say this is the time of night when ghosts are most active. Was it a Borden ghost calling out from beyond the grave?

CHAPTER 4

HAUNTED CONNECTICUT

Connecticut became the fifth U.S. state on January 9, 1788. It is called the Constitution State. Some people also call it the most haunted state in the country.

The Old State House is a National Historic Landmark. These historic places are important to the nation.

In 1647, Alice Young was found guilty of witchcraft. She was hanged at the Meeting House Square in Hartford. The Old State House was later built in its place. It became the state's first capitol building in 1796.

Today, The Old State House is a museum. Many say it's haunted. Doorknobs are said to turn on their own. Ghostly footsteps sound up and down the halls. Early one morning, Ronald Bolin was working at the museum. He heard voices coming from the Senate room upstairs. It sounded as if people were having a meeting. Bolin took the elevator upstairs. As soon as he stepped off the elevator, the voices stopped. The room was empty.

WITCHCRAFT FEARS IN HARTFORD

The fear of witchcraft swept through Hartford 30 years before Salem. A young girl became ill and died in 1662. Her family said a neighbor had used witchcraft to kill her. Soon, the fear of witches took over the town. Four people were put to death.

Many of the stones used to build the prison weigh 1,000 pounds (454 kilograms).

A stone wall was built around the prison to keep inmates from escaping.

OLD NEWGATE PRISON

The crumbling Old Newgate Prison in East Granby has seen a lot of history. It was constructed on top of an old copper mine in 1773. Underground tunnels were turned into jail cells. Prisoners often ran away. Their cells were dark, wet, and crawling with rats and lice. A few prisoners even died there. The prison had to close in 1827. It was too dirty for prisoners.

Today, the prison is open as a museum. Visitors can walk through the tunnels the criminals called home. Some say the ghosts of former inmates never left. People have reported hearing ghostly screams. They come from down in the mines. Some visitors say they feel like they are being watched. One visitor said their group's tour guide was dressed like an inmate. The visitor later thanked other employees for the tour. But they said no tour guide was working that day. Had it been a ghost?

One of the most famous haunted places in Connecticut is Dudleytown. The small village was established in the mid-1700s. Farmers and ironworkers moved to the village. It seemed to be a good place to live. But then, the town slowly died. The last residents left in the late 1800s.

Some people say residents left for better opportunities. But others blame a dark force for what happened to the village. The Dudley family was one of the first to settle there. They were said to be cursed. Stories say anyone who lived there would also be cursed. According to legend, many villagers died untimely deaths. Some are said to have gone insane.

THE WARRENS

In the 1970s, ghost researchers Ed and Lorraine Warren visited Dudleytown. They said the land was overrun with **demons.** They took photos at Dudleytown. They said the photos showed strange swirls and streaks. Others had **orbs**. The Warrens said this proved the land was haunted.

Abandoned towns can be hot spots for ghostly activity.

Today, all that remains of Dudleytown are a few old foundations. Signs warn people to stay away. But that doesn't stop some thrill seekers. Many visitors say the land gives them an overwhelming feeling of fear. Visitors report all kinds of eerie happenings. They report ghostly laughter and whispers. Glowing orbs float among the trees. A woman named Sarah and her friend visited in 1998. As they drove closer, Sarah's back began to hurt. Her friend felt pain in her stomach. They parked and climbed out. As they walked, the sound of scraping metal rang out. But they were the only people there. The friends left in a hurry.

CHAPTER 5

FORT KNOX

Fort Knox sits along the Penobscot River in Prospect, Maine. This military fort was built between 1844 and 1869. Union soldiers trained there during the Civil War (1861–1865). Today, Fort Knox is a state park. It's also said to be haunted.

No one was ever hurt or killed at Fort Knox. But many visitors say they've experienced ghostly activity. Strange laughter has been heard when no one else is around. Invisible hands touch visitors. A ghostly soldier is said to haunt the fort. Many people believe it's the ghost of Leopold Hegyi. He was the caretaker from 1887 to 1900. He spent much of his time at the fort alone.

HAUNTED NEW ENGLAND

New England is the oldest part of the United States. Many famous battles took place there. Important people called New England home. Some say its long history has also led to hauntings. What do you think?

More than 100,000 people visit Fort Knox each year. Some leave with spooky stories.

DO YOU BELIEVE IN MONSTERS?

- **45%** of Americans believe ghosts are real.

- **45%** of Americans believe demons are real.

- **13%** of Americans believe vampires exist.

- **46%** of Americans believe in otherworldly beings, such as aliens, angels, and fairies.

Based on a 2019 yougov.com poll

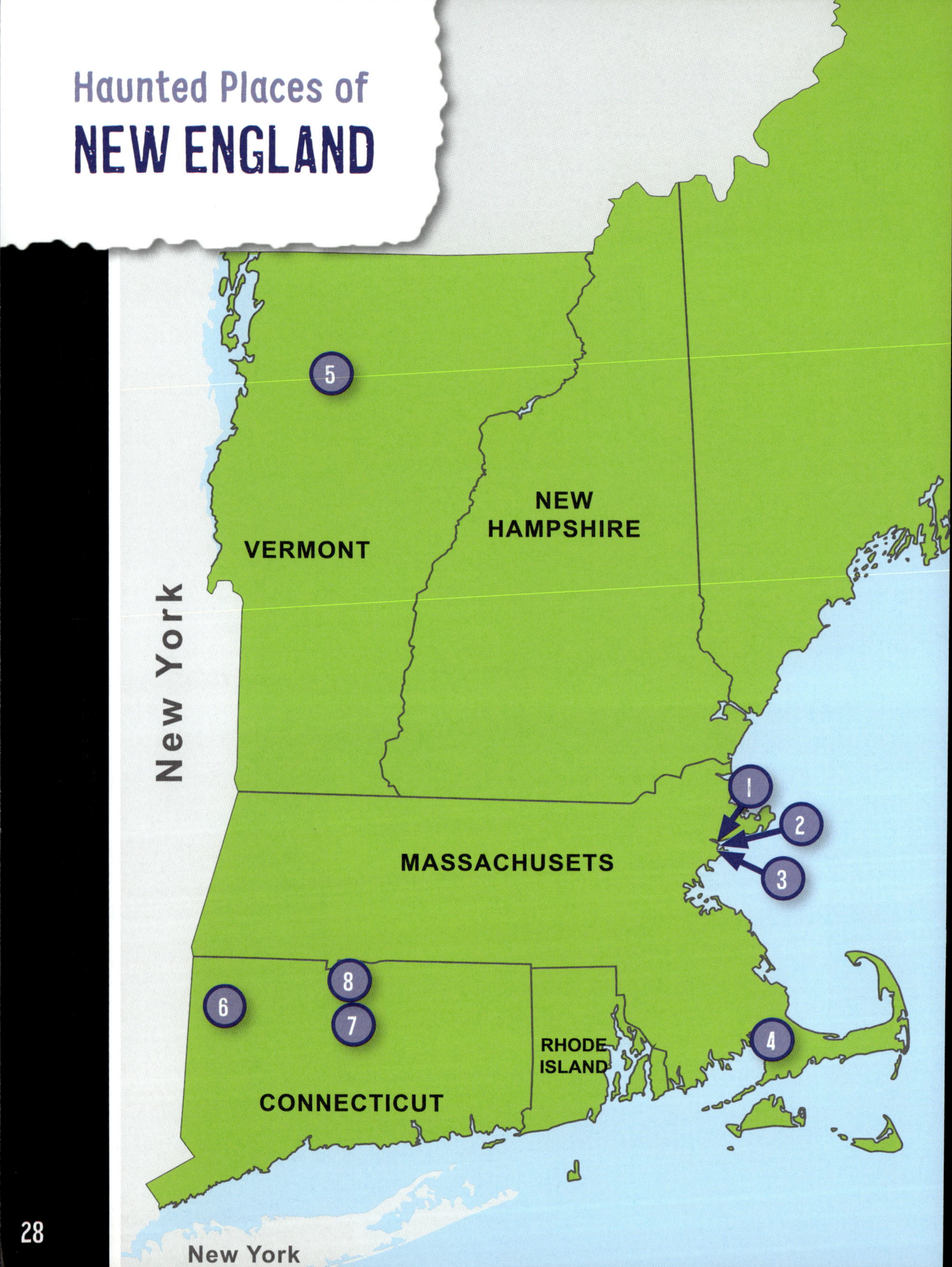

Haunted Places of
NEW ENGLAND
VERMONT
NEW HAMPSHIRE
New York
MASSACHUSETS
RHODE ISLAND
CONNECTICUT
New York
5
1
2
3
4
6
8
7

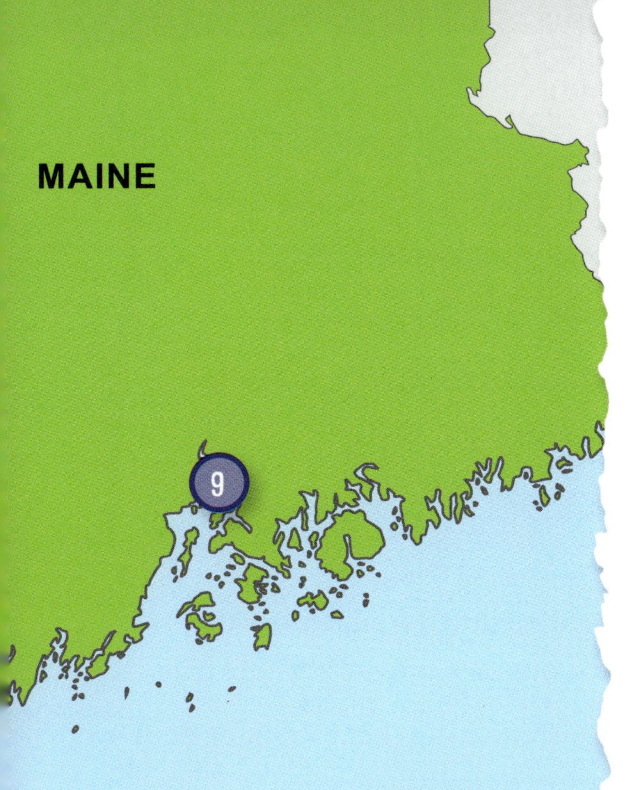

MASSACHUSETTS:

1. **Old Burying Point Cemetery**
2. **The Corwin House**
3. **The Joshua Ward House**
4. **The Lizzie Borden Bed and Breakfast**

VERMONT:

5. **Emily's Bridge**

CONNECTICUT:

6. **Dudleytown**
7. **Old State House**
8. **Old Newgate Prison**

MAINE:

9. **Fort Knox**

GLOSSARY

colony (KAH-luh-nee)—a territory settled by people from another country and controlled by that country

curse (KURS)—to lay an evil spell on someone

convicted (kuhn-VIK-tid)—judged to be guilty of a crime

demon (DEE-mohn)—an evil spirit

jury (JUR-ee)—a group of people at a trial that decides if someone is guilty of a crime

legend (LEJ-uhnd)—a story handed down from earlier times; legends are often based on fact, but they are not entirely true

memorial (muh-MOR-ee-uhl)—something that is built or done to help people remember a person or event

merchant (MUR-chuhnt)—a person who buys and sells goods for profit

orb (AWRB)—a glowing ball of light that sometimes appears in photographs taken at reportedly haunted locations

suspect (SUHSS-pekt)—a person who may have committed a crime

READ MORE

Burgan, Michael. *The Salem Witch Trials: Mass Hysteria and Many Lives Lost.* North Mankato, MN: Capstone Press, 2019.

Niver, Heather Moore. *Are Ghosts Real?* New York: Enslow Publishing, 2017.

Wilkins, Ebony. *Perron Family Haunting: The Ghost Story That Inspired Horror Movies.* North Mankato, MN: Snap Books, 2020.

INTERNET SITES

Fort Knox Historic Site
https://www.maine.gov/mdot/pnbo/fortknox

Six Historic Haunted Houses in New England
https://www.newenglandhistoricalsociety.com/6-haunted-houses-new-england

The Salem Witch Trials
https://kids.nationalgeographic.com/explore/history/salem-witch-trials

INDEX